BOOKS BY DENISE LOW

NEW AND SELECTED POEMS

2nd Edition

DENISE LOW

PENTHE
Middletown, California

Distributed by Mammoth Publications
www.mammothpublications.com

Dedicated to my husband Thomas Weso and our families.

Poems originally appeared in these books: *Tulip Elegies: An Alchemy of Writing* (Penthe, 1993); *Vanishing Point* (Mulberry, 1991); *Selective Amnesia* (Howling Dog Press, 1988); *Starwater* (Cottonwood Press, University of Kansas, 1988); *Learning the Language of Rivers* (a *Midwest Quarterly* chapbook); *Spring Geese and Other Poems* (University of Kansas Natural History Museum Publications, 1984); *Quilting* (Holiseventh Press, 1984); and *Dragon Kite* in *Mid-America Trio* (BookMark Press-University of Missouri-Kansas City, 1981).

The poet is grateful to editors James Gilkeson, Michael Annis, George Wedge, Stephen Meats, Gina Bergamino, Philip Humphrey, Linda Samson Talleur, and Dan Jaffe.

Uncollected poems appear in the following publications: *Spud Songs,* eds. Gloria Vando and Robert Stewart; *New York Street Reading Series Anthology,* ed. Carl Calvert-Bettis; *Poets at Large: 25 Poets in 25 Homes,* ed. H. L. Hix; *Phoenix Papers,* eds. Stanley Lombardo and Steve Addis; *Midwest Quarterly; Controlled Burn; Sycamore Roots; Potpourri; Primary Point; Cottonwood; West Branch; Kansas Quarterly; Soundings; Helicon Nine Reader,* ed. Gloria Vando; *Roberts Foundation Awards Anthology,* ed. Stephen Meats.

Cover photograph: Terry Evans, "Mixed Prairie Grasses, Konza Prairie," 1979.
Original cover design: Jim Gilkeson

2nd Edition

ISBN 0976177366
Penthe Publishing, Middletown, CA

Distributed by Mammoth Publications
1916 Stratford Rd., Lawrence, Kansas 66044
www.mammothpublications.com

Contents

New Poems, 1999

New poems in this collection come from as long ago as 1989 and as recently as 1999. Some are from a book, *Lacunae,* which was never published. The misadventures of that manuscript illustrate the complexity of publishing poetry in the corporation-dominated book business. Three small presses accepted it, and all ended book publications before *Lacunae* was completed.

Most poems, though, are from 1996 to the present. These are a group informally titled "Postcards." Travel is their theme, and the surprise of the tourist experience. Work and family take me to odd corners of the state—and the world. I spent several weeks during summer of 1997 in Thailand visiting my son. When I returned, I found Kansas exotic in its own way. I began writing Kansas "postcards" as well.

I continue to find poetic topics based in this region. It is like no other place, and few people understand the experience. The media continue to stereotype the Great Plains—like the quaint scenes of rural America in *The Wizard of Oz* and *National Lampoon's Vacation.* What is missing in film images is the quality of space. The sky expresses infinite moods, including, at the horizon, the possibility of alchemical union. On a human level, people have more space to manifest their imagination, and each community has individuality.

I appreciate the local support I have received through a quarter century of publishing, support from readers, editors, fellow artists, and arts agencies. The Lawrence Arts Commission helped pay production costs for this book. Penthe Publishing continues to produce books.

The Bear Emerges

Sky shudders with first
thunder of spring. Bears
shake themselves and rise
to the voice above
and together, bears and sky
make a new year begin.

In bed we hear the rumble,
distant, as we find again
under blankets and skins,
the deep-set thud of heartbeats.
All through the hard winter
we forgot about rain and lightning.
We lived alone except for pines
and a solitary cardinal. Now

as the day comes to life
we think of bears awakened
to sky-drums and wild onions.
We think of their growls
and claws scraped over bark.
We open a window and wet air
breathes into the house. Again
we are alive, again we are all alive.

Timber Creek Trout, Colorado

In clear water a trout learns the art
of camouflage. Along the cobble streambed
it turns into a sunken stone, or when sun
magnifies the clear current, it hides
in the past: its shadow does not move.

Sometimes it appears in disguise
as a drowned tree root that flickers
then settles back into midnight quiet.
Only a pale disc illumines its ceremonies—
wordless courtship and launching of eggs.

Above, on the surface, sun chases shapes—
splotches of trunks or patches of brown fur.
The fish circles safely below in washouts
hidden under the bank. A frigid watery nest
holds the last of winter's chill. Brief summer

lasts as long as the western sun, then fades
behind the mountains. Frigid air returns
until frozen spray encrusts the waterway.
The trout floats through underworld channels
where it suspends, where it shadows.

Cup and Saucer Hills Drive
Cowley County

Wild turkeys startle us. The tom
unfurls his feather bustle and poses
while the females scratch grass.
His cartoon face signals alarm
even as you touch my cheek.

At the bridge we stop again
and watch the current. Inside
the deepest pool a shape emerges
from rocks and turns into fins.
Sudden carp lips snatch a strider.

When the mound looms over us
it is no more surprising than
our rollings together called love.
The wrought-iron gateway says
"Cup and Saucer Ranch" in black cursive.

On the saucer hill sits the plain house,
and inside the upturned cup shimmer
steel fencing and pickups and wet cattle.
That fish, a sucker, had a bizarre
clown-yellow mouth, and the turkey gargled.

All the day seemed implausible just as
we fit together like crockery,
like calligraphy, like rain pouring
into a cup-shaped hill—or flesh
shaped like a bird and a fish and a man.

Council Grove on the Santa Fe Trail

Riffles show water interrupted
in the flow of river. We, too, stop
for the night and find a room at the hotel.
We enter an old story, as people

who meet at the river, water horses,
cut timber, drink and sleep.
For centuries people used this grove—
the last hardwood trees before Mexico.

The layer of insoluble Neosho flint
under the current is solid footing,
a rippling ford. Cottonwoods also gather
on the banks and past them, tomorrow,

we will enter our own sky-blue myth.
We walk on dry paving stones raised
from the river. We find the hotel key
to our room and our last night together.

Billy the Kid stayed here and Bill Hickock
at the bar we will smell women's breath
as we swallow whiskey from old glasses.
Walnut beams will hold up walls of the past.

Tomorrow Custer's men ride North to die
while we turn South to find the rest
of our lives. When we leave the Neosho
wind carries the smell of dried oak.

Another Coronado Heights Story

The sky here reminds me of that Indian guy
who dated my sister, the bookish one
who drove his dad's red Thunderbird
and later wrote a book about Lake Kahola—
a Walden-Pond experience about winter,
Thorovian except for wind and Ndn humor.

Later he married and moved to Lindsborg
near the knoll where Spanish camped before
they turned to more likely goldmine country.
I once heard a Pawnee named Echohawk talk:
how Pawnee fighters defeated the Spanish
how Pawnees held the Republican River.

Years later farmers plow up pieces of armor
near Coronado Heights and spurs and bits.
The museum in Lyons has a good collection.
My sister's old boyfriend was restoring a hotel
near there when he died at Coronado Heights.
Perhaps he decided to disappear into distance

for a purpose but real life is not romantic.
That night he was out with friends drinking,
not into any vision, when they ascended
that hill. It rises singularly from wheatfields,
a stepped pyramid to the sky. They paused.
Then on a downward curve he went airborne.

His wife remarried. The hotel became a bed-
and-breakfast, with a Swedish smorgasbord.
Coronado Heights still stands hazy-blue.
At least, in that night's pause, he saw stars
from the Heights. He should have written about it.
He should be the one telling this story.

The Town of Hoxie

Five hours west into the high plains
Sand Hills break against sky
like frozen surf. Fossilized backbones
from dinosaurs appear like half-finished giants.
White road stripes are their vertebrae.

I arrive in Hoxie as the snow begins.
Two highways cross here. Cattle trucks pass
and pickups with gunracks. In a diner
men wear muddy rubber boots that reach
to the thigh. Pies are homemade
and the lettuce trucked in from Denver.

"Hoxie" means "drunk" in Choctaw
but I am sober when I read the menu:
*Fresh Ostrich Steaks. From a Ranch
in WaKeeney.* The waitress asks
if want it rare or well done.
She serves it with A-One sauce.

Fog descends, the solvent of distance.
My hands are magnified and breath is white.
Sky fills with chunks of ice
and the highway becomes a snowy river
with no bridges. On either side lie wrecks
of old monsters, hulls of metal or bone.
I move slowly among them.

Kansas Grasslands
for William Stafford

Big bluestem around us quivers,
alive as horse manes seem alive in wind.
This is the grass Stafford wrote about
as though it were "the sky" or "forever"

only this grass changes colors, mauve
by the Wakarusa River, and yellow,
and by roadside the bleached fox-tail grass.
Grass seed bundles brush against sky,
their long-tied knots loose at last.

We track deer, not Oregon whales,
in these waves, but still we drown
under eight-foot stalks of bluestem.
Switchback grass, too, splays
fronds overhead, like eagle-feather fans.

This imperfect circle is Stafford's horizon,
a curved line to keep stars from spilling,
a quill-stitching through air, a thatched edge—
the path he traveled skyward and back.

Haunted Falls, West Virginia

On a cold spring day we find the falls,
the Cherokee name lost except
for the translation *Bad Spirit Falls*—
a place where every summer suicides
and careless teenagers fall into chasms
among sandstone boulders and disappear.

On shore bluets color the shelf-rock
and ivory blossoms of blood root.
The water churns North, pulled
by the dropping channel, snowmelt
sent back to its homeland. North
is the direction of witch trouble.

I learn the story of a man brought
back to life. *Here his wife washed him
until his flesh was whole again.
But still he dies. He needs the spark
of other people's lives. At night she rises
from water and finds souls for him.*

I keep my footing, careful on the gravel.
Shadows move underwater but no fish
or turtles. Hidden at the foot of the falls,
buried under moving water strata,
lies a bowl of sandstone, glittering,
solid bedrock, bright as the full moon.

Flint Hills Sunset, Spring Equinox
for Tom

This could be the first night of creation.
Beings lie just under the earth's surface
about to take form. Enormous skulls press
taut against the hide of grass.
Falling twilight flattens everything
into silhouettes. Rounded dark shapes
are babies still within their mothers.

Only mammals will be born in this world
with long flanks and frizzled surfaces.
Lumbering bears do not quite arise.
Buffalo humps rise halfway
but they are not yet animals with horns
and brown-agate eyes. Red-tail hawks
wait for dawn before they settle
within cottonwood trees.
Mice fold within thick dry grass.

Nothing is visible as cold wind
blows on a blank, pitted planet surface.
We can create anything here and forget
when Spanish traders came or Kaw Indians
or the sunburned cattle drovers.
Lapping stone ripples the crust
as Sun turns the last horizon molten—
and all the shadows sleep.

Postmodernism in Kansas
If it is Einstein's brain, what's it doing in Lawrence? Lawrence J-W

Diane Willie decides whether to speak
Navajo, English or Keresan Pueblo
as we drive a stretch of the Oregon Trail
now called Highway Fifty-Nine
and filled with drunken sports tourists.

She asks about Einstein's brain in Lawrence,
a one/twelfth section kept after the autopsy
in 1955. Dr. Harvey works at E&E Displays
and loans out the brain sometimes,
like for a Japanese sci-fi film starring

William S. Burroughs, who lives
on Learnard Street behind chain links.
I recall dinner with him last spring
and conversation about smart worms
trained to crawl mazes, then chopped

into pieces and fed to other worms
who crawl the same mazes without
being taught, and then he said,
"Einstein's brain is in Lawrence"
and smiled. He wore a bowie knife

and used it to slice chocolate candy
and egg rolls but I wondered if
he liked brains, maybe scrambled
with eggs, and now Diane asks
as we drive through slow Kansas stars

"If William Burroughs eats Einstein's brain
is that what 'postmodernism' means?"

Elegy for July 28

Cicadas ratchet against air
as sun withdraws from
the garden leaf by leaf.

Dark collects around flames
of the first fireflies.

Sycamore leaves lie still—
dark banners against trunks
of white-bark trees.

Downtown the Gods of this day
lean against a wall

with the old men and talk
until the last light and then
dissolve into stonework

their faces flattening against stone
as though they never existed.

The Fallacy of Travel: Letter to Bruce

Here in the center of fields
and low hills where surf crashes
only in fossil limestone,
the great silence around me

is a lie. After twenty years
I finally know, old friend,
I was not left behind.
This shelf of rock soars

through wind and sine waves
of time. I watch buildings
appear and collapse. Trees
I planted stretch up and fall.

There is a noise, too,
I hear in bed at night,
a drone deeper than cicadas.
I hold my husband close.

We read Rilke together
and listen to squirrels
thud on the roof and apples
fall and our brass bed,

on casters, rolls forward
at the speed of starlight
and the walls move, too,
at the same speed, fast,

much too fast,
and this only seems solid,
this quick night here,
now, as I remember you.

Mornings I Never Leave You

Mornings a misted road opens
its slow arc through floodplain.
The Wakarusa River tosses
somewhere south in the midst
of willows and osage orange.
To the east, Blue Mound rests
from its slow erosion as air
filters over it. The sun illumines
each hill, each piece of stone.

These mornings I rise from bed
and leave your solid back.
I leave the warm skin you fold
over me against cold and
the blotting of night.
Sun consumes tail-end darkness
as I drive into small changes:

grackles ornamenting a tree,
grass winnowing the wind,
white dew sifting back into sky.
Traced by distant branches
the Wakarusa,
a small river I barely see,
loops through wet silt,
holding Earth in place.

Flathead Catfish

Catfish as big as men wallow
beneath the dam, rearranging rocks
to fit six-foot bulge of torso,
head and tail. These monsters
have whiskers covered with taste buds
and nerve lines down their length
to sense movement across the river.
They live through seasons unchanged
as the mud, indistinguishable
from rock outcroppings, clay-brown
and just as still. Open mouthed,
they wait for bass and crayfish.

When a man drowned, his wife
walked the banks for weeks
alongside the pool of flatheads.
At last she called psychics
to séance with water and spirits.
They probed other worlds
but heard no voice rising
from currents or sinking into
bottomless sand. They sensed
only a presence at nightfall,
a stirring when catfish awaken,
when night animals come to life.

Sycamores and Herons

1.
One cold February
the stars tilt South again
filled with new light
and settle into lake ice.
By the shore
a stand of sycamores
makes a brilliant roost—
white-barked, with snow
crusted on limbs.
A heron barely appears,
blue wings crooked
over moon white-feathered nestlings.

2.
The pain of sycamores:
at dawn they grow and the skin
does not stretch but breaks
into pieces and drops away. Yet
along the river—ivory, the shape
of antlers—see them rise.

3.
Wind strips old leaves and they
cover ground like stars.
Behind them giant bones stand
where owls wait out
the long night of winter.

Deer Magic

Phantasms:
they appear
by stealth
and disappear.
They shift into vision—

    glimpse of antlers
    dark tails
    and then gone
    the air empty.

In the wetlands
we find a print
cast in deep mud
weighted by a rack.

I believe in them:

    mottled bodies
    not quite formed
    in mist then
    rain clouds
    drop over us all.

Winter Count

On his birthday I drive my son to soccer.
On the asphalt strip spanning to the horizon
our Ford arcs over glacial bedrock.
With the other cars we are small.
Late winter, and the sky folds turquoise
against fields and last year's grass.

On the radio K.U. falls behind St. Johns
but Cedric Hunter passes to Danny Manning
and Danny scores. Eighty to eighty-four.

This is what my days come to
and a dream last night
of a basketball hoop jammed into limestone.
My warm-blooded son spun
and dunked it, but sideways.
It was hard to tell which way was up,
scrambled with fossils in stacks of ocean rock.

This cold afternoon we are queer fish,
flipping and diving through wind, radio waves,
white sun, and dreams of who we are.
Midway up this stone planet my son counts
his fourteenth journey around the sun.

A Phoebe Arrives in March

For Bob Antonio

Artisan of air, the songbird
rises over telephone wires
and pumps wind through wings
and throat. He slings notes
like invisible fencing around
rivers and cottonwoods.

Morning sounds are spells
to raise sun-gods into heaven,
two tones to weave hope
into chains of generations
like grass strands twilled
through foliage and flocks.
Worker and lover and singer—
he voices and re-voices the sky.

Dragonflies
for David Dotson

Sunfish—aquamarine and topaz flashes—
ellipse beneath muddy water. These

are the best part of fishing
and the dragonflies.

While the bobber floats in its puddle
of stillness, dragonflies bask

on the line and dazzle—
their wings filled with waterfalls.

Green darners, skimmers, and black ten spots
are elegant hunters of the river.

Watching them is better than facing
a shock-eyed fish, hooked in the lips,

gills bloody. Stories say fish
have no nerves and feel no pain.

I cannot believe this. When fishing
the long wait is the best

cloud shadows passing over
and my back against a willow trunk

Water edges into cattails and among them
aqua needles pierce sunlight and shine.

Scenes from Emporia

1. Bas-Relief

A few thousand people breathe together
night-quieted air, an invisible rhythm.
Time recharges under old stars
as still air settles deep
between frame houses and elms.
Earth-black miles surround town
and stretch into bottomless fields.
Sky bears down so hard
the town is held motionless.

At the downtown intersection
the only awakening will be
the train whistle, faint at first
like a distant coyote whine
coming from the farthest, darkest edge,
then moving closer, wind rushing in,
whistle filling yards and sidewalks,
closer, marking acreage of night
all the way to the center of now.

2. Atchison, Topeka and Santa Fe: Arrivals

The train is a thread
drawn through the town
east to west
and the town itself
a needle's steel around motion.
Whistles, grinding brakes,
each brick of the walk
shaken in dirt
and I know

lines of track
will arrive soon
rolled up in boxcars.

The old black engine,
iron rhinoceros,
bellows
and my father climbs down
heavy-footed on dry land

smelling of coal.
He carries a canvas bag
and inside are pieces
of other lands.

One time he hid me aboard
behind the twirling beacon.
I could see the light
skewer blackness
and tracks aimed west
like a moving ladder.
We made our escape
on that bolt of lightning.

The stationmaster did not
catch us that night
and all the towns fell behind.

3. Night Walks

On the pavement, time slips backward
to children's long afternoons
of wagons and trucks and marbles.

One yard tells a story of an iron gate,
hedgerow, bricks, goldfish pools.
Overgrown honeysuckles scratch glass.

Next door a porch of wind chimes,
glider, geraniums and cactus—all
assembled for an outdoor parlor.

Against the side window
organdy curtains frame
the yellow lamplight glow.

In the lighted pane, gray sleeves
move and stop. Hands appear.
Then nothing again but lamplight.

A back yard dog barks,
pauses, barks, pauses, pauses, barks.

4. Hometown Scene

North to Sixth Street I see last week's
tornado damage—a telephone pole snapped
in three parts, new Fords wadded, but
it's old news. Traffic moves, and sky.
Afternoon sun fires a clump of yellow iris
at the corner of Sixth and State.
In the distance a man walks toward me.

Driving down Twelfth Street I see
the brick street, dust blowing,
a shirtless man still walking.
Clouds follow him east. Downtown
in a room above Stanley's Jewelry
one corner window catches the glare
like yellow heat trapped in topaz.

5. State Street

Back then the street
was a great strange river.

Our house was safe
but through that road flowed

kids, people dressed for church,
parade floats and once

a horsedrawn wagon, plain wood,
and even then I knew

the brown horses and old man
came from a distant place

I would never see
back where the world started.

The old man held reins
in twisted hands, stared ahead,

turned and disappeared
like a secret.

What I knew was my corner
and the sign's black font:

Twelfth and State—
this far I could count.

Flint Hills Elegy

Sunrise again.
Lightened clouds
and a few geese appear
mixed among stars and fog.

My father died
and does not see
this wan light
create cattle ponds
and grassy slopes.

He does not see
the gray streak of highway
leading westward, upland.

Black night slips into
the last horizon.
The firmament brightens.

Beyond the dark edge
of these fields waits
another ocean of sky
far west of here. At night
it will swallow the sun.

Making the Bed

Here are tangled sheets, bodies gone
but castings remain of thighs, torsos—
traces of the night. Wrinkles
reveal where his crooked arm pressed
the mattress, where my hips
bore weight, where a pillow fit.

All are indistinct, blurred suggestions
like a deer appearing roadside
out the corner of an eye, undifferentiated
from night except for fluorescence
of golden eyes, the smudge of brown fur
and quick—the image disappears but
left behind cloven wedges crimp silt

as we imprinted the bed, formed
and reformed against each other's skin
and feather pillows. Then we dreamed chaos
behind our eyelids—old houses
and forgotten streets of bricks uneven
where an old creekbed ran. At last

we rise from the night bed and forget
heavy scents and our long embrace.
We forget constellations distant
over the roof—dimmed animals turning
in their firmament: swans and small bears
and the hunter Orion after them, running
forever through the dark and resting only
when light quiets the sky.

Holiday in Clinton, Missouri

In the parking lot a john boat scraggled
with dried grass must be a duck screen—
a float for the hunters' parade
but on concrete it is a withered monster.

At the lake a heron has no fear.
It rests in the shallows until
we walk into caked mud too close
and its flapping wings blot the moon.

Inside the waitress serves grits and beer.
The band leads dancers through songs
about love and divorce. This
is like the town where I grew up

just a hundred miles away,
the same accent but the vowels
stretched longer, and when the waitress
calls me "Honey" I cannot find words.

How To Read Petroglyphs
for G. Barnes

Imagine never seeing
a book, a North-side-up map,
billboards or street signs.

Tree trunks will look round again
and veins of leaves
no longer are flat rubbings
of Second Grade crayons.
Then travel into Utah,
into red rock mountains shifting
against clouds and ornamented
by sage and scarlet sumac.

Violin music comes to mind,
Bach arpeggios, as we walk
into a box canyon—a concerto
of boulders and hollows.
At once the carvings
live in our vision:
> *sheep*
> *crosses for stars*
> *spirals*
> *stepped mountains*
> *foxes*

Above, the ghost moon
rises through broken sky.
Blue air and blood-red stone
fit together like a scale
leading back to the first voice
and the first hand on rock.

Two Gates

I look through glass and see a young woman
of twenty, washing dishes, and the window
turns into a painting. She is myself 30 years ago.
She holds the same blue bowls and brass teapot
I still own. I see her outline against lamplight;
she knows only her side of the pane. The porch
where I stand is empty. Sunlight fades. I hear
water run in the sink as she lowers her head,
blind to the future. She does not imagine I exist.

I step forward for a better look and she dissolves
into lumber and paint. A gate I passed through
to the next life loses shape. Once more I stand
squared into the present, among mango trees
and scissor-tailed birds, in a Thai garden, almost
a mother to that faint, distant woman.

Lotus Garden
for the Wakarusa Wetlands

The fetid ponds
turn magical: pads
overlap silk-floss knots
of buds, striped cerise,
and then one arises—
a Buddha figurine
come to life within.

Minnows flutter
inside dank shallows,
and eddies where bass
attack water striders
and fall back, turtles
raise question-mark necks,
and herons dip beaks—
the cacophony of feeders
under parasol leaves.

Lily roots seek
the anchor of mud
and spew sap upward
into explosion of silk,
each bloom a quiet saint.

Traditional Massage
for Jim Gilkeson

A woman half my size. Upstairs, open windows over the street.
Fans and TV downstairs. The spiral staircase twists up. Backwards
trousers I change into.

Futon mattresses on the floor. She pulls and cracks every knuckle of
my toes. It does not quite hurt.

She uses her bare feet like hands. Her toes are thumbs.
They walk into deep muscles of my thighs. They arrange the coins
of my spine.

Hands on each side of my pelvis, she bears down all her weight.
Bones are a stone-rimmed bowl she cannot flex.

From behind she hugs and lifts. She bends me forward into halves
like a folded blanket. She unfolds me.

I have been this close to few people. She is not a lover nor can we
speak. She learns my leg muscles and slight curve of forearms. She
learns the tension of my neck. I feel her breath.

She leans on my knee joints and ankles. They loosen. Deep thigh
muscles come alive.

We spend a lifetime together. She travels from birth to death.
Toes to scalp. It is always this final moment at the end of all days,
upstairs, over the street.

One summer we are finished. I return to the mattress and sit up.
Where she pressed, still, the imprint.

Whale Watching: Farallon Islands

Now my grown son is a well known
stranger. We go whale watching
together, close again as we were
when he was small and never
left my side. Whales swim

in family groups. From the boat
we see two adults, their spray
smelling of sea-plants.
They steer through waves and dive,
spotted flukes the last sign

before they disappear. We lower
binoculars and I sense
underwater movements like giants
rumbling through a cavern.
The ship monitor shows knolls

below, in a rocky landscape.
The boat motor is too loud
to talk over but we wait together
until they rise to the surface and blow
exhaled breath alongside

and again the grassy smell.
The procession of behemoths
meanders, and our wooden boat follows,
slapping swells, an awkward cousin,
clumsy on the ceiling of their world.

Abyssal Zone—Monterey Bay

for David Low

When old sharks die at sea
they drift through kelp forests
into abyssal deeps, a cold storage
where dragon fish and angler fish
light the way and transparent jellies,
lit from within, their clear bodies
the only echo of sun. Pressure builds.

Sounds would be unbearable clatter
against stretched ear drums
but no flicker remains in bodies
as they settle into cold hell,
eyes open but at rest,
flesh as uncorrupted as saints'

while aloft, on some surface,
mussels bore through rock
and in shallow waters
anchovies glitter like one body
broken into a million pieces.

California Potatoes

The Peruvian restaurant served
everything with lots of rice
and chili sauce. I ordered quinoa
and purple potatoes dotted
with goat cheese, a mounded
plate, steaming, and the potatoes

were firm, as sweet as fruit
but also meaty, meat from a plant,
the strength of rocks and soil
poured into tubers and saved
underground for this moment,

this bite into an apple of the earth,
into the histories of Incan and Irish
and Senegalese and Pakistani—
all peoples who cook potato morsels
in lamb stew or curry or salad
in peanut soup or chowder or latkes.

Here by the Pacific these Spanish
and Incan people come North
along the coastline, accompanied
by potatoes, like underground fish—
lumpy and slow, inland a few miles,
but always on the move. My fork

presses into white flesh and I taste
all their centuries. I smell
the Andes Mountains and coastal
salt-winds, and my stomach fills
with earth and air and stories.

The Trip to Paradise

California, starts at Grizzly Peak, winds down Berkeley hills and then flattens toward Vacaville. I read a Babel map at 70 miles an hour. Next comes a confusion of back roads that do not exist. Radio speakers speak in low tones about tree care and straight sex. Then Arabic voices speak, maybe from Eden, and then German, Spanish.

A stop sign appears at a tee intersection and neither path will go north. The car turns into a bank of fog. Rural mailboxes on posts appear, with red flags. The wrinkled map does not trace this two-lane highway ending at a bridge.

Then the ghosts start. Not the Scottish kind that step out of portraits and walk castle hallways, nor the old woman in my living room who sits in a pressed-oak rocker. More nebulous. A quick ache in my thighbone. A cry in the distance. When the headlights hit one farmhouse, I can see the wife's face trapped in a window pane.

Then silence. Not even eight o'clock and it is deep night. I feel rather than see the elevation rise. Hills are blocks of pumice and volcanic craters worn down to ridges.

Up Skyway Road I see streetlights and more roadsigns. My headlights pierce mist, where mesas float in the heavens. Stars fold into black clouds but reappear.

But the mountain can not be predicted. Roads switchback into spirals that angle into other dimensions. I look in the glove compartment for the emergency map, the exact size of the road, as the car soars.

Pacific

Fins flicker within waves, peaked
like water itself, interchangeable
with whitecaps, the same shape repeated.
Waves turn to flesh a moment and then
ebb into nothing.
               "Harbor porpoises"
they call rolling shadows
slipping out of sight and then
they call them "sea lions."
Here I understand death, how eyes
disappear under the surface and
change names.
               Fat murres
float on swells, startle, and churn
thin wings. Somewhere one
sinks into the depths again.
Everywhere we see gulls and cormorants
They carry in their feathers all
the possibilities of gray.
               Afternoon lengthens.
Clouds descend from the sky
to walk the watery plain. A sea lion
face appears in a trough and nods
the same rhythm, and we breathe together
the same salt-heavy air. We feel
night winds quicken from the south.

Lake Superior

I am alone. No sign of anemones
or tidal gust of kelp. No saltwater. Just
a sweep of biblical still waters,
and between the halves of the world
the thinnest, barely-discerned horizon.

Shades of cloud overlay the water:
blue-white, gray-white, violet-white—the colors
dissolving on the lake's surface. Last spring
ice vanished but its trace lingers
in the quiet. Phantoms of frozen blocks drift
in the depths. Fish are winter shadows
who shift and disappear.

Finally, above, a single goose
flies into the prism of twilight,
bleats a single sound into widening circles
of distance and beats its wings through mist
stroke by stroke, until it is only blur and echo.

Spring Equinox, Wolf River

Even here sparrows
cheep in the background,
a netting of plain song,
the warp and weft one color,
a constant note sounding
behind our conversation.
Back in Kansas sparrows
speak with the same voice,
wear the same brown coats,
unremarkable. Two beaver
swim below the bridge,
snout first, cleaving dark glass
until they slip under ice,
as silent as the fading light,
and the Wolf River lies quiet
this cold spring night.
*

The shore of land
merges into ice
where fishermen stand.
Pike swim
under their feet.
An island of trees
stands connected
to solid river.
An eagle rises over
birches and wings
up river, the only
motion—and then
our minds hold nothing.

First Night

I did not know what I chose
that first night, except
you warmed me. I waited
for you to turn back but
your mouth found my shoulder.
You walked that last half-step
and fit into me.

I waited for you to find
my temper inside
but you pulled me
within the tender inner arm skin
and held me there.
I still feel that enfolding.
Parts of that night I remember,
like your cheek pressed on mine,
but nothing remains permanent.

I thought of losing you
even as I first touched the seams
of the delicate lines where
skin turns to red fabric
of your inner body. We slept
and we did not sleep. Night
did not end. I still feel
the tether of touch,
the presence in my muscles
where you anchor
against me and hold on.

Vanishing Point, 1991

Poems that became *Vanishing Point*, published by Gina Bergamino of Mulberry Press, were whimsical. No particular thread ties them together besides a sense of play. The forms are variable, and looking back at them now, I find these were experiments. Most did not find any more formal publication than this small, twenty-page chapbook.

A difficult part about writing poetry is learning which pieces are only personal and which may have a place in public discourse. I value how these commemorate a spell of equilibrium. I enjoyed friendships with fellow writers and artists in Lawrence, especially members of a writing group—Judith Roitman, Stanley Lombardo, Steven Addiss, Caryn Miriam Goldberg, Jane Hoskinson—and friends Roger Shimomura, Carolyn Doty, Luci Tapahonso, Bob Martin, Norman Gee, Stanley Herd, Kenneth Irby, Wayne Propst, Jim McCrary, Michael Annis, and others. I enjoyed conversations with William Burroughs, as well as stories about the writer's Lawrence life from close friends.

The first poem, "Ceilings," shows satire of Midwestern ways. However, by the end of this book's span, my father had a crippling stroke and became aphasiac. I began commuting to hospitals, a rehabilitation center in Topeka, and my parents' home in Emporia. The last poem, "The Language of Aphasia," is a precursor of *Tulip Elegies,* and the tone is much darker.

Bergamino published chapbooks in Wichita and then moved to New York City, where she continues to publish Mulberry Press.

from Vanishing Point

Ceilings

Teepee smoke holes
lead sleepers into heaven.
Dreamers can float up poles
to distant starts overhead.

Cathedral vaults sprawl for blocks
of imitation halo-tinged heaven
with gold-leaf angels and saints
for penitents to anticipate.

Methodist ceilings are flat.
The steeple calls townspeople
to worship but inside
heaven is plain white plaster.

Lobby ceilings of banks rise
as tall as granaries—
square-cornered, trimmed in brass:
giant, closed chests of treasure.

Schools have ceiling tiles
with tiny round perforations
to soak up wandering minds.
Children trace multiples of twelve.

This room has ceiling lights
and around them space where words
collect all day until switches
turn off and all of us disappear.

Mice in the House

walk around us while we bathe
or read the newspaper or quarrel
over hot water in the bathroom.

Mice invade the stove
chew up the insulation for nests
and pop out of the top burner
when I'm on the phone and can't scream.

Mice chew holes in the garbage sack
and the fifty-pound bag of dry dog food
and the baseboard under the TV.

Mice hunker down in carpeting
while we read The Nutcracker
about the Mouse King with seven heads
and how Clara's shoe knocked him dead.

Mice leave trails of what my mother
called Mouse Dirt!
in kitchen cupboards and under skillets
for me to find in the morning.

Mice hear my bad thoughts and run
through the house with them
frightening the sleepy house.

Alone at night, reading in bed,
I hear their restless chewing and know
every bad wish I ever had
is alive in walls, floors, and attic.

Friday Nights
for Helen and Norman Gee

One time the plattered pig
with Farrah eating the eyes
Roger the cheeks and ears,
and the rest of us the limbs.

Another time we consumed
Arvin's hand-raised steer
diced, marinated and offered
like a lost friend.

In spring we ate morels whole,
smoky and wild labyrinths—
emissaries from the Underworld
sautéed in butter and wine.

We talked, yes, and drank wine
as we chewed forests and meadows
seas and reefs—
as we became one flesh.

The Language of Aphasia
after The Hanged Man, a tarot card

Since his stroke it is as though he hangs
upside down, gagged, his four limbs crucified

on the dimensions of time and space. He speaks
only simple syllables, beginning with m-m-m-m

and finishing with open vowels. He has
this survival-level language, a child's

first alphabet to reach for milk or mother—
and with these simple sounds he gropes

to describe the terrain he floats in.
When I promise he will speak again

he shakes his head no. He breathes sounds
through his lips, squeezes them flat

and open, and then stops. I tell him
he will heal and learn speech and one day

rise from the weight of unmovable flesh
where he flounders, struggles for air,

and invents a new vocabulary
as though his life depends on it.

Tulip Elegies, 1993

Tulip Elegies is the first book I did in collaboration with Jim Gilkeson of Penthe Press. Jim and I had known each other in college at the University of Kansas, and we had remained aware of each other's lives through friends. When he returned to Lawrence from Germany and decided to start a press. He asked to look at some of my recent writings. The tulip poems suggested relationships to him that I believe, reminded him of homeopathy tenets. My research about tulips led me to connections with the plant to alchemical principles.

I began writing this series of poems after reading Susan Fromberg Shaffer's wonderful poem about tulips, and also another one by Sylvia Plath. This was in the fall, and I was indeed planting bulbs—actually daffodils—in the front yard. My father was in a rehabilitation center after a stroke, and this weekend I stayed home to focus my mind on life instead of loss. The first tulip poem, a hopeful elegy, came to mind.

My father had been a vigorous, opinionated, intelligent man, and overnight he lost the ability to walk, to feed himself, to read, to talk, and to sit upright. Although he lived another five years, the man I had known as my father died. There was no funeral to mark this passage. I did not directly write about this transformation, because it was still incomprehensible. The elegaic poems began to emerge during journal writing.

When Gilkeson saw the tulip poems, he asked about the process of their composition. The essay about the poems, which is in the original book, is a result of his encouragement.

from *Tulip Elegies*

Tulip Elegies

I.
November, season to aim
the spade and bear down hard.
Grass gives and rips open:
sod and black flesh.
From crumbled stone will rise
the new year. I bury
crisp buds into the breach
and press them further down.
Decay surrounds these children
all winter like memory surrounds
each moment. Next March

shining petals will carry
a core of darkness up from subsoil.
Sun will loosen wrappings of crimson
and tulips will show open hands,
empty, as though nothing spun
in their centers all those months.
Skin and layers of muscles enfold
the same spinning shadow,
the mystery passed from parents
to children, in far places,
in graveyards where life begins.

II.
Geese bleat over the roof, conversing
somehow with stars as we drowse
beneath constellations of beating wings.
Rearranging staggered lines they steer
a sunward pattern, calling out
as they fly, naming the long way.

Below, under shovels of dirt
the dead move imperceptibly,
turning into other shapes of life.
Tulip bulbs shift under dark horizons
of winter and wedge against years
of decayed shale. Shoots form within,
still trapped, and a miniature blossom
waits in each bleached kernel. Last spring
winged leaves fed this future and wilted.
Now, unmoved by geese or moonlight,
bulbs listen through solstice nightfall
for the searing call of one hot star.

III.
Some of the bulbs interred last fall
with handfuls of bone meal will freeze.
I held each bundle—paper wrapped
around pear-white flesh—and set
each into cold soil to grow or die.
Now, in a winter room, under quilts,
I touch my husband's longing. I understand

nothing about this, not the tulips
settling underground and maybe kindling roots
nor the magic pull, like lodestones,
that draws my husband to me each night.
Wound between sheets, skin laid against skin,
we create heat and salt and quiet deaths:
unseen children bleed away. Still

at the center of midnight we come alive
and sense the force that creates us
and geese and next summer's grass and one day
will pull us down into dark histories.
Formless, we become more like a tone
bowed on a cello, *sostenuto*. At solstice

nothing appears to live as wind scours
the hard rim of ground. The new year,
buried below the frostline, is imagined,
is a small hope no larger than my hand.

 IV.
Each stalk forms itself
with the symmetry of Bach,
pulls green blood up
into latticework of cells—
augers headfirst
into windy blast
and sun dazzle.
Relieved of the burden
of soil, hard-edged
ruffles relax
and uncover their end—
the single striated bud.

The blossom will balance
over earth, stiff stamens
and smudge of pollen
within a heart-red cup,
the shape composed
to fit between stars

and rock hinterland
where bulbs vibrate
unseen, unheard,
earth-anchored.
The planet's fiery center
pulls, contrapuntal
to the thrust of growth.
It holds fast
each stem aimed
into weightless sky.

V.
This shining in my chest—
familiar, painful, a yearning
to bust loose from skin
wrapped around me long ago
like pearl around a seed
yet the luminance is turned
inward—some fire hung
between my throat and belly
to burn and pull me onward
to a lover and to children:
the part of me most unseen
and most potent.

The one-chambered tulip bulb
becomes an ember underground,
a charged lump within pieces of dirt.
From one milky center
covered by tunic and scales
will explode a full-grown plant,
a replica of Dutch ancestors
and Turkish "turban" flowers.

A tracing of its pattern hovers, invisible,
the arabesque of growth held ready
for when the sun turns North again
and sets continents ablaze with petals.

*

Each funeral ends and we remain
alive, with each other, still
in love, still held together
in a veined framework assembled
from old stars. This existence
is not our choice, nor are the sun
and ground we live between.
The burning in each of us—

dormant bulb or human heart—
strains beyond lips and fingers,
beyond evenings spent together
talking into the quiet evening.

The desire to change soil
into petals, that certainty
seared into the oldest bulbs,
is familiar, is a charge
even in my red pulse,
a passion in sap or blood:
I cannot sleep alone.
My shape carries a heat within,
counted out in rhythms when we kiss
and when springtime, I see
a fresh tulip—scarlet, full-fired.

VI.
Vial of saturated color
sculpted from peat,

red red after winter light.
Curio: emperor's tulip.

Living Faberge egg
rubied by dawn.

Aphrodisiac for the sight
and light touch.

Most perfect lover,
softest lipped, fullest curved.

Centered in the garden
or elevated over bread and meat:

ornament of symmetry
domesticated to fit my hand,

to fill my table with solid
geometry and music.

Fragment of sunset
still radiant at midnight.

Faceted garnet. Tamed dragon.
Catch—of my breath.

VII. *Tulipa hermetica*
The caduceus of lily-flowered tulips
rises from ancient humus—
a bouquet of stems and black eyes—
and renews the memory of gods.
Petals collect particles of gold
by day, dark silver by night,
then shatter back into earth.

Below, where serpents nest,
all the dead intone one word:
everlasting. Without stars,
time erodes like granite.
Roots seine the underworld
and gather strength for
the yearly pilgrimage to light.

Each year's sun moves quickly.
Emerald daggers pierce sediment,
burst into red petals and die
while hidden bulbs swell with buds.
Two-bodied tulip, hermaphrodite,
weds sky and black earth,
mortal blooms and eternity.

VIII.
Resurrection is a falsehood.
The Danish man buried in peat—
stomach filled with spring seeds,
cord around his neck—did not rise
and return to his old mother.
Only barley and rye came to life
as swampwater seeped into his veins.

The *penitente* in New Spain
nailed to a pinewood cross
as cousins guard the highway—
this young man will not revive,
gash himself again with thorns
and offer blood rosaries to Mary.
His last sight will be red dirt,

particles of mountains and roots
stewed together with snowmelt.
Mud is where miracles occur,
where blossoms, kings, and wolves
come apart in final union.
Last Year's tulips disassemble
with stripped bones and clay.

New buds this spring are not
the same flowers resurrected.
They are strangers, never before
seen, born just this once.
Petals are fragile butterflies,
brief spans of tissue to measure
only a half-moon life.

Bulbs live on below, secret,
safe but alone, mothers
who sacrifice all their children
while they become hard knots

and endure. Each year they barter
with the dead around them, swell
with new hope and wait.

IX.
A place camouflaged
by summer grasses,
but underground, hidden:
a fairy ring of spores.
Mussel-shaped buds
folded within tulip bulbs,
embedded in haunted gardens.
*
Snakeholes shaped by stems, abandoned,
running sap dissolved.
tunnels carved out
like dry creekbeds,
storms ended, twisted
by single-minded current.
*
Not simply a wizened husk
and pulp, but some future
wound into a vegetable
locket, some clock
waiting to be unsprung
by cold hours, water,
a star's close pass.
*
Ghost stems and flowers
left to hover
among chilled roots.
This black season:
muffled sleet above,
hard frozen roof,
and within—held breath.

X.
Alchemy means darkness: *Khem*—
old word for Egypt—means
black earth. Flooded fields
and graves where losses conclude
become the alchemist's furnace,
like Nile Floodplain, sun-stewed
limned with soil and salamanders.
Putreficatio begins

and the King sinks underground.
He joins serpents and worms
and His purple robe blackens.
He roams onyx mansions
and does not see His tears
steamed by sulfur and fire,
or a leafy wreath around His head
rise uncorrupted into heaven.
From hell He calls to the sky
but His lips cannot make sound.
His body has turned invisible
except in shadings of black:
in oakwood smoke, in grooves
of carved stone, in inkwells,
within closed books. Inside
dark blood He pounds and pounds.

Bone Alchemy

*"Man incorporates death into himself
with his bony structure." Rudolf Hauschka*

Philosophers' stone lies
hidden within skin—
bowled pelvis and skull.
Old bone surrounds
the "scene of life's creation"—
the red marrow sea
where elements turn
to life. With each breath,
water turns to pith.

Flat circles of spine,
too, are crucibles
where blood is stirred
into being, a miracle,
as the alchemist touches
chalk flask and fires
the furnace. All night
tincture is distilled:
salamander red.

Selective Amnesia, 1988

Most of my work avoids personal disclosure, especially of painful experiences. *Selective Amnesia,* a chapbook published by Michael Annis of Howling Dog Press, includes metaphoric references to emotional struggles. These were the shadow side of my writing during the time I also was writing hopeful poems about river life, published as *Starwater.*

Some *Selective Amnesia* poems were based on personal stories, and others on stories I had heard from friends. Also, I had been researching the Ice Age glaciation that shapes the landscape near Lawrence. The common thread among all these topics is the cold indifference of time. Species come and go, like the woolly mammoth and giant sloth. These surreal animals once existed in Kansas. Maybe the lost mega fauna represent my own monsters—the part of my own nature over which I have no control.

I remember getting the call from Annis that he wanted to publish this set of twenty-five poems in *Stiletto I,* his new magazine. I was spending a summer in California, where I felt dislocated anyway, and his call seemed especially unreal. I had met him, his wife Alison and their sons at the time of the River City Reunion (1987). This was a celebration of William S. Burroughs' residency in Lawrence. Many writers journeyed to Lawrence for the festivities. Michael commemorated the event with an amazing portfolio of broadsides. He then assembled artwork, the writing, his own graphics and text design for *Stiletto.* I was privileged to be included in it.

from Selective Amnesia

Selective Amnesia

I step down into
the museum basement
like I've done dozens
of times and finally see
the duck-billed dinosaur
running across the wall on
tiptoes, bones turned silent.
The skull crest is a misplaced
bishop's miter maybe filled
with tunnels for air or sound.
The eyeholes are voids,
the jaws a hinge of blades
held in the solid rock coffin.

All other trips down these stairs
I overlooked it, another blurred
wall pushed aside for years
forgotten except for
flickers in monster movies
and dreams where I am chased
by something unseen
and when I reach the end
I see piles of bones
laid down in rocks
and something invisible rises
high on its toes
about to catch me but
I jolt awake.

Evy Survives the Winter

Raking out dead leaves I see
what has lived through this winter.
The blue ajuga is gone, and most of the pink,
but chrysanthemums send up lime-green doilies.
A cardinal's whistle nags over and over,
circling the tree canopy, invisible,
no longer a scarlet trill against white snow.

Across town this afternoon Evy paints
her story into a journal, pictures of dark times.
Her brush moves across a white page
and moments from thirty years ago appear
sharp in the sunlight, uncovered, bright red.

A Kickapoo elder told me wisdom comes
when we look behind us
and recall each day back to red birth.
That unbroken line makes us whole.

Evy paints. I clean the garden,
piling leaves under the pine tree.
On bare ground, iris fans open.
Snails inch back to the rock pile
and a new season begins.

Late Winter Night

The furnace lunges into life, heaving
through vents, and the hound inflates
and exhales, dreamless. Outdoors, the last
winter sunset, brilliant baboon-pink, tumbled
off the edge of Earth, into absolute dark,
and it, too, breathes somewhere, unforgotten.

I sit motionless in a pool of lamplight.
No crickets scrape wings. The silence seems
unmovable, yet we all hurtle through meteors
and seasons, the well worn track.
Already time to burn the Christmas tree.
Even if I sit very still tonight
Siberian crocuses soon will pierce frost.

The whole house, wheezing, lurches,
and from this midnight I am carried forward.

The Garden of Maternal Amnesia

She knows this is the day
to transplant iris.
She notices marigolds
push off from dirt and build
towers of orange thumbs.
Caladiums bare
baby-pink hearts to her
and zinnia beds are green lips
about to speak.
Day lilies sing
from soft fleshy throats.

Next winter African violets
will sun themselves
and grow cheeky leaves
on her windowsill.
The scarlet amaryllis
will trumpet Noel.
When she answers
a long distance call
she will talk about
hard freezes,
precipitation
and bulbs buried
below the frostline.

Ogallala Aquifer

As the water table sinks
mid-range rivers falter.
The Arkansas River loses its way
to Wichita. The Smoky Hill
lapses into gravel
and long stretches of silence,

like Heraclitus, muffled,
only fragments remaining
from his distant writings.
Or Sappho—her broken
songs are beds of old lakes,
just the outlines visible
like wheel ruts
of the Oregon Trail,
almost imaginary traces
across grasslands.

These river beds make roads
out of smoke-blue hills.
Cobbles follow and sand.
Far underground
the Ogallala aquifer,
a lost Ice Age sea,
dries into solid stone.

Pray for the People
for Chava

My sons light Chanukah candles
one, two, three, four flames
and our friend recites Hebrew blessings
Black solstice night cloaks the windows.

Flickering light ends this hard year.
We still see
        Cheyenne people at Sand Creek
        Jews of the Holocaust
        murdered Cambodians

and our friend beside us
        raped by her insane father
        all through her childhood
        and bullied and beaten.

Somehow the candles are a healing.
Her voice rises over my sons,
over their slender, fragile bodies.
Soon they will grow into men
sure and strong enough to be gentle.
The first word we taught them,
while touching the cats, was "gentle."

        May they live this next year as children.

        May this Chanukah heal us all.

Cartography
for Ed Ruhe

The ring-necked snake
chooses a narrow range
and sticks to home rocks,
nosing out long earthworms
within an oblong territory
the shape of its own silhouette.

And does the turtle see
round scenes?
Does it up-periscope and see
spokes converging towards its hub,
its own splendid hump?
Does it gaze upon concentric circles
arranged like an English garden?

Maybe the best mapmakers are Australians.
Each slight rise in the Outback
hosts a Dreamtime spirit and story,
the design of land refracted
through the human retina.
Even in the starkest stretches
an Aborigine has map and compass,
gospels to follow all the way home.

Body Memory

Even after amputation
a phantom foot
can be pinched
or chilled.
No medicine
soothes away
invisible pain.
      Amnesiacs
still feel in their flesh
what happened even when
their minds hide from themselves.
A body never
blanks out but binds
each taste into cells
and blood.
      Years after incest
a woman feels her body finally
release the aches and terrors.
It lasts for months,
her body telling its story
the only way skin can speak
and be heard.
      The knee
for example is dumb but still
remembers pleasure or pain,
permanent markings
sinewed close to bone.
      Truth
is not in philosophy
but in animal hide, teeth, and meat.

Starwater, 1988

As my sons grew older, I found myself traveling the Kaw River valley with them, sometimes by canoe. We walked the sandbars and floated into backwaters where great blue herons fished. The river transformed into a different being each time I entered her realm. My dreams became rivers and rainstorms. Late spring weather lasted indefinitely. Poems came.

Starwater is from the balance between my own inner world and the world of the river. I started a series of poems called *Learning the Language of Rivers.* I sent a few to Steven Meats, poetry editor of *Midwest Quarterly,* and he asked if there were more. I am grateful to him for his mentorship. He helped me push language into natural patterns, like the scallop-ridges left by water running over silt. He published the series as a special poetry chapbook within *Midwest Quarterly* 38.4 (1987).

The sequence of water-related poems continued. I traveled in Utah and wrote about the Bear River. I continued to dream about the Kaw and the Neosho River, where I grew up. The story "Yellow Woman" by Leslie Marmon Silko, which I taught in classes at Haskell, stayed with me for days. I felt inhabited by a water spirit.

The next year, when a book-length manuscript accumulated, I asked George Wedge of *Cottonwood,* the independent literary magazine and press affiliated with the University of Kansas English Department, if he could publish the book. He agreed. Don Low, my children's father, contributed part of the printing cost, and again, I thank him.

from Starwater

Starwater

Nursing my first baby
I drank eight glasses of water,
two quarts each day. He grew.

I felt like a carrier for water,
passing it on through to the child,
and some day his child, too,
will fatten, remarkable
like peaches and muskmelons
leaching juice from bare dirt.

Astronomers tell us star dust
once swirled together,
cooled into rocks and water
and still circulates,
the same matter pulled into stars
and Earth and into our flesh.

So water travels the skies,
stretches into clouds,
and falls, moving ever East,
circling, the same ancient water
caught in the whirlwind
binding us all together—
gravity, or maybe
as we know it, love,
or water drawing together all its kin.

Inside the River

Spring rains rushed beyond this spot,
changing sand into petrified waves
and sudden drop-offs
dug back at angles into sift river belly,
the random deep holes of whiskered catfish.

Springtime is stopped here in grainy patterns
interrupted only by a few heron tracks
and framed singularly in the ripples:
fragments of bisque crockery, skeet traps,
whiskey bottles—stories from western counties
all carried into the current,
spun around, broken apart, and suddenly found
years later, miles away, down the river.

Summer River

I am drawn back to the river
as though it were the grave of a grandmother.

Hot summer skies uncover the sandbars.
Another season's tide of floodwaters recedes.

Near the river appear new talismans—
pearl-plink mussel shells, chert, beaver fur—

beached on the ribbons of sand and water
that wind through miles of muddy cornfields.

The river is a soup of histories.
Deep sea limestone from the Pennsylvanian

mixes with mastodon teeth and plastic lids.
Old sofas spill their guts down steep banks

and abandoned cars go nowhere nose down in mud.
All of it means something I cannot fathom.

Each summer a new set of clues
arrange themselves, as in dreams:

always changing, always moving,
never completely certain.

Yellow Woman

The river is a woman of yellow sand.
I lie down in her, leaving a print
of hips and breasts. Soft water touches inside me.

All afternoon I lie under her skin of water and sunheat.
Her brown body dances in all directions.
As we travel, unmoving, closer to dusk, I understand

I would follow a lover down crumbling banks
to warm sand and lie with him,
leaving behind even the children

I would wash him in river water,
our hair smelling of willows. We would fall
asleep and remember the woman,

Yellow Woman, who fashions sand into catfish,
who spreads over a man and tastes
his ears, his teeth and lips, his sweet salt

as sticks float down the current, and cottonwood leaves.
We would forget everything but this river
that carried us into life.

Little Piney Float Trip
for Jim Bogan

Wizened mountain stubs rise around
a young river. Water pulses by,

polishing gravel at our feet. The chert is ivory
the color and size of teeth, cast-offs

from these bluffs, Ordovician.
Humming water unravels monuments

and we lurch into the current.
Many years we have loved each other

and rivers. Once you sent dried piranhas
from Rio Negro. I send regular reports

of the old glacial river, the Kaw.
Now our hearts beat here, in this boat,

dodging shelf rock and shallows,
passing a bottle of wine,

talking of scattered lovers,
children, and our stubborn art.

We pass Mill Creek and swallowtail butterflies,
trestles and rock bass. We slip finally

into twilight and the Gasconade,
swallowed by a whale so smooth

we hardly notice. Already it has happened.
Dear friend, the river undoes us again.

Another Tornado Dream

I am near Wakarusa River,
a rope of brown water centered
within wide terraces.
This valley marks
the ancient glacier's
southernmost margin.

This is the place a tornado
touched down in 'eighty-one.
The cloud moves away,
still formless,
but then it doubles back.
It explodes into a waterfall of wind.

In the dream I remember
a tornado will not touch
the fork of two rivers,
but I am miles from a confluence.
I crouch by a forked tree
and wrap my arms around it

as though it were a father.
I can feel the tree
is a force, too,
like wind and water,
like the river of ice
that once bulged this valley open.

I pray to the tree so intently that I awaken.

Summer Drowning

Just a moment to step into
this delicious high summer current
cresting with all of spring's thunder.

A smooth coverlet slips over
my ears and eyes. No terror.
A release into silence and heartbeats.

This river turns corners so widely
I can ride forever a long wave.
The channel buries itself deeper

and deeper into farmland
and I follow.
Up on the sliding surface

sunlight shimmies
on polished brown glass.
Everything is hushed and waiting

like a child holding her breath

and counting how long

she can stay under.

An Ice Age Ghost Story

The death of the Kansas glacier
still shapes our river this evening.
The Kaw bends around invisible ice
as the western sky turns lavender and gray.
Dismembered Ice Age animals swim in sand,
brilliant snow-white bones
turned porous and umber.
They sprawl, scattered with driftwood:

horses, boars, giant beavers, and mastodons
wash from a lost graveyard
and travel from Lecompton to Lawrence.
On the voyage
they give themselves piece by piece
to the mineral kingdom
and become clinky, bone-shaped rocks.

Tonight I will lie next to my husband,
fit my shoulder just under his,
my arms next to the sturdy box of his ribcage.
Hot winds will spread up the river valley
and stir grass outside our window.
Before drifting off we might speak of
the lost spruce forest, the ice,
the lives of all those bewitched beasts.
We will sleep in warm coats of flesh.

We Wait at the River
for Denni Doran

My son knew you would be gone
along time because we took you to say
good-bye to the river, just below the dam

where whitewater shoots fish through sunlight,
gulls sharpen against sky and in winter
an eagle clan gathers for a good catch.

Here my sister once asked what the smell is,
always, by a river, and I said fish, but
it's more—that smell we remember in winter

and even miles away where you must be,
the smell of mud and turtles and olive catfish
still alive, hours later, in the sink.

It's the smell of Mary's Lake, late autumn,
and the boys start a smoky fire. You tell us
about the nerve line down their sides,

how they can feel any vibration, and their sense
of smell. When even one fish is taken from water
they all know. Territories readjust. David

has grown since you left and I wish you could see
the river with us again. Channel cats glimmer deep
here, under bridge lights, waiting for shad.

The Same River, The Same Good-bye

for Ian Edwards

1.
I have my Ice Age bison tooth
from the river and you
a mastodon tooth and a Folsom point
discovered buried in a gravel bar.
We have had the pleasure of hiking
across sand spits and imagining
what lies beneath the water,
sunfish or clownish bullfrogs or fossils.

Now we both travel to distant country
with river relics,
reminders that everything changes
on the Kaw River or the Rhone
yet even change comes in familiar patterns,
like generations of buffaloes and elephants.

This year, under the same brimming sky,
each cottonwood leaf disappearing
into mud or the flat-faced river
forms a splendid, yellow heart.

2.
Leaves drop again this year,
cottonwood harts and maple hands,
small deaths.
But where each stem separates
there is next spring's bud.

In this city of concrete and traffic
mice find my house,
and in the same sycamore,
each fall
an owl.

Through downtown
the river moves as usual
pushing driftwood
past city hall,
past wintering eagles.

Each fall
a horizon of tree trunks
rises around the river
gray and unmoving
and yet still alive.

In this familiar forest
the river is an unfinished edge,
an unraveling rug,
shapeless water running
as fast as it can
to the next season
to the next living container.

Pilgrimage of Eagles

I dream of eagles winging over the river
and know northern waters are frozen shut.
The same band of eagles returns
to cottonwoods on the Kaw.
They forgive us our cities and persist,
following open waters just past the edge of ice.

Each year we journey up River Road
to watch them circle clouds like Gods,
drop, and take fish.
They silence even the children.

When snow arrives from the northlands
they appear and enter our dream.
We sense them for miles away—
like geese flying over at midnight,
voices calling from just beyond conversation.

Eagles bring sleet, a curtain of darkness:
the long season of what remains
after wind strips away familiar summer.
We learn to listen for them
in the dark, in the quietest moments of sleep.

A Snapping Turtle

Not the squirming one,
fighting fingers
at the end of fishline,
mouth bloody and curved beak ready,

not this hooked outlaw
but the one on a bleached log,
eyes hooded against the glare,
its orb, rough hewn, set to rest.

This turtle stays in mind
and the river in repose
like it would last this way forever,
like I could understand it finally

unmoving—the green Neosho muffled
and filled with sun,
silent dragonflies
and a sleeping snapper

that bit deep, years ago,
into my young eyes
and never let go.

Enantiodromia

Another man drowned in the river
below the dam, his spirit held
under the rocks until he joined
the others—sand, turtles, and carp.
Sleeping in his boat, too late
he found the current no dream
but more real than his mother
and children. He tumbled calmly
over the dam, braced only for a swim.
Downriver his friend popped loose
but he settled under the river,
quietly, with the minnows.
Light gradually dissolved.

This killer river gives birth each day,
flowing across town in pipes.
People bathe in it, wash clothes,
and water all the dogs,
dumbly alive, and we wonder
at this man plunging into lifeblood
of the city while squirrels chew seeds,
leaves breathe, and a pregnant woman
folds the last of the laundry, sighs,
and drinks deeply from a glass of water.

Robert Smithson's "Mirror Displacements"

"Sight consisted of knotted reflections bouncing off
and on the mirrors and the eyes. Every clear view slipped
into its own abstract slump."

      A snail scouring the bank
does not really see, but tastes,
in its own fashion, and touches
textures others can only imagine.
Fractal geometry, measurement
of shoreline to the most specific
degree, is its specialty. No wonder
the coiled tape measure on its back
is saved, filled with memories of waves,
slick stones, and silicate facets.
It ever so slowly understands
each equation moist under its tongue—
particles of silt, black wood, glass.
It leaves behind its trail of study,
a glazed meandering polygon
shaped to its own kind of sight.

*

"Outside this island are other islands of incommensurable
dimension. . . . The memory of what is not be better than
the amnesia of what is."

      Swimming out to a sandbar
only a fraction of the river laves
the child's chest, thrashing feet, and arms.
This becomes apparent some seconds
later, since her brain is only a crude
chemical mirror floating in miles of river.
On the sand, looking down into the dimension

of fishes, she casts shadows from heaven. Perceptions
capsize. The horizon becomes "an enchanted region
where down is up." She twirls in the sun,

wet arms held horizontal by centrifugal force
and wet hair shedding a sparkling river.
The idea of Atlantis opens in her mind. She
becomes an island washed by reflections from sun,
water, mud, and something else behind her eyes.

*

*"The island annihilates itself in the presence of the river,
both in fact and mind."*

      The river surface mirrors sky
and destroys it, fragmenting clumps
of sunlight and rain clouds.
Where sky touches quivering edge
of water, blue air disintegrates
into oxygen molecules for fish.

Where the river touches bottom appears
another slow decay of shale into mud.
Each dawn scattered over current repeats
a slow erosion of the heavens.

In Martin Cheng's Studio
for Nancy Zimmerman

Three fish lie flat on newspapers.
Streamlined sides and fins are useless on the table

yet scales still reflect moments of river sunrises
and the mystery of animals shaping themselves

from water and mud. An artist must paint
this fast, form translucent washes and fluid

calligraphy for each scale and each point of light.
The newsprint can be done later, but to capture

these shining crappie Martin's brush swims
in water and pigment as quick as minnows.

He moves fast, flicks his full brush,
smokes, sings, dances to the paper and back—

lumbering land movements, clumsy
next to the sleek glide of sunfish but maybe

the closest we come to moving with river and earth,
the closest we can come to grace.

An Agate Charm

1.
They are slow clocks like tree rings:
mineral-charged water settled
into a lava bubble, layered
around a center—the eye.
Four thousand years measured each band
and always an escape path
where water seeped in and out
like a Navajo blanket
always left with a thread undone
for spirit to slip out and away

like time.
The Aztec god of time
propels the earth:
his eyes stare out from
the calendar stone.
He commands fire, earth, time, and
heartbeats of the world
repeated over and over.

Like agates—
each one, too, a center and a beat,
calendar and map at once,
carnelian or copper or violet,
rainbows collecting around a pivot,
layering year after year,
faithful to stone laws.
          May your life grow full around a center
          like this agate.

2.
Agates sit on the shelf
as you and I talk circles of words
of mothers and fathers ahead of us,
our sons to follow,
the layers of generations
we lie packed against
and can never change.

Past years are seed pits within us
we do not leave behind
but carry deep
like mussels sealing over pain with pearl.

If you want to extract a sorrow
wrap it with a stone
and throw it deep into Lake Superior.
Water rings will hold it tight,
and you can choose a new road home

like thread leading the spirit safely
out from a Navajo blanket
or the passage leading out
from a mother's full belly
or the path outward
from an agate's eye.

3.

Like agates:

apricots, chalices, breasts, mandalas,
bulbs, jewels, eggs, sun and moon,
tree rings, water rings, rainbows, pearls,
the circle where earth meets sky.

Like agates:

bird nests, raspberries, water jars, cocoons,
geodes, snowballs, sunflowers, acorns,
eyeballs, nautilus shells, teapots, rosebuds,
the planets in their orbits.

May your life grow full around a center
like an agate.

The Physics of Waves

1.
Each morning I defy gravity,
wake up, will my body to rise
vertical and speak. No one has

explained this:
the simple dawn and I awaken.
Midnight and I lie unconscious,

dreaming, I think, a hibernation,
flat along the earth's pull,
maybe aligned with it, grounded,

like an airplane, for eight hours.
So waves on the river rise up
lifted by wind, form brief wings

and then fall back into place.
Their appearance of travel is false.
All afternoon watching waves

lap against sand, really
the same water peaks and falls back
with no choice but to rise when blown

as sunrise burns my eyelids open
day after day, and black night
pulls me back down to earth's center,

a lake of liquid hot stone.

2.
Mostly we are space.
Each molecule contains only tiny
bits of atoms, and within them—
maybe only a hiss of motion,
a tiny crackle of something
neither matter
nor energy.

Mostly what we see
is illusion, melded pictures
of isolated points.

All the empty space
of our bodies floats
everywhere we go
even within
the pressure of rushing blood.

Gravity tugs hard.
Its pulse binds
our bodies,
the moon,
the rivers,
and the empty parts
in between.
It keeps cars
on the streets and walls
from toppling over—
this mirage of solids
where we keep coming alive,
pulled together into rhythms
of shivering
breath.

Flood Stage
for Beth Scalet

1.
Beth said being crazy was like
total telepathy, knowing what
her friends were about to say.
Their secrets filled Beth's mind.

Last night my lover called out
in his sleep because he was melting
into everything, like rivers
enlarging and spilling over roads

and bridges—simple water,
hip deep in the fields, forcing itself
into fragile outbuildings.
This spring my dreams flood

with yellow water, the dangerous color
of tornado skies, something out
of its place filling the streets.
The car stalls. My way back home

is blocked. Then I know everything
about floodwater rising against gravity,
but I do not awaken.

2.
The spring we met, it rained
every day. We made love long
afternoons, upstairs, surrounded by
turning branches and streaming water.

We gave ourselves up
to gray light sifting
through window glass.
Pigeons murmured beneath
layers of rain.
We learned the first
lesson of death—
flesh falls away.
We floated high above
the trees the roof, above
two lovers tangled in bed.

North of town the Delaware River
crested and blurred into the Kaw,
a spinning river
falling fast down
wide slopes of prairie—
   weeks later tumbling to the Gulf,
   on a day we awakened together in sunlight.

Spring Geese, 1984

This collection began as a set of poems about the University of Kansas Natural History Museum. When I took my sons to classes there, I wandered the halls. In the exhibits I found an education about Kansas that never occurred in any formal instructional setting. The book takes its order from the museum itself.

I appreciate many aspects of my schooling, from diagramming sentences in Mrs. Carle's eighth grade class to the M.A. in literature I received from K.U., 1974. However, only in a junior high class did the Kansas surroundings seem, briefly, worthy of study. Especially the omission of significant Kansas writers like William Allen White (from Emporia) and William Stafford (BA and MA from K.U.) seems incredible now. Victor Contoski was my introduction to poet William Stafford.

Wes Jackson writes about how the Midwest is the place most Americans emigrated *from,* and so now they see it as backwards. Few KU professors are from Kansas, or the Midwest, because of the practice of not hiring local people. So the distance remains between writers of this region and the academy.

As a stranger in my own land, I began to look for the exotic "other" in my own yard. I remember Gary Snyder's 1977 visit where he stressed involvement with local geo-politics. He, in turn, was influenced by Charles Olson. Osage poet Charlotte DeClue challenged me to get involved with the local Indian community rather than perform "missionary" work for distant Indian causes. I began teaching at Haskell Indian Nation University in Lawrence in 1984.

from **Spring Geese**

Flight

Fossil birds are the rarest,
their delicate span of bones
crushed in heavy folds of mud.

Their meat was too sweet
hollow bones and feathers
too light
their wings
too fast for floods or volcanoes.

At the museum we have
some pterosaurs stuck in shale,
a few sharp-toothed loons,
one contorted bat.

The rest are an invisible flock
still in flight.

Spring Geese

Not one tidy vee
but a whole complex of angles
branching off each other
like a genealogy.

Spring, not fall,
and this is Kansas,
not the northern wood.

Not a magazine cover
of migrating geese

but their honking chorus
spread across the southern horizon
stays in my ears for day.

Niobrara Shark: A Lesson

Shark bones sprawl in a slab of chalk —
fifteen feet of stony ribs
hung against the museum wall,
and impressions of pumice skin,
mottled rock, the grainy seabed.
Perfect rings of cartilage and vertebrae
shape a wandering line of spine.

Halfway back floats the last meal,
chunks of backbone and spiked jaw,
a puzzle of broken fish.

Best preserved is the shark's head:
some skull, jaw, and a tumble of teeth.
Triangular, serrated tools,
edges jutting into our air,
shining stones hooked into dull bone,
shark teeth—
amulets of long life.

Sparrows

Summer solstice.
Birdsong surrounds us
through the sun's fullest circle:

rising spirals of bell tones
from the catbird in the pine,
chucking from blackbirds.

Brown-capped sparrows
send out simple words
over and over,
their whirring throats
as busy as water:

measures of sound
spin into a fulsome sky.

Rolla to Lawrence

Red-winged blackbird
dead on the road
six miles out of Rolla.

Opossum by the Gasconade River,
teeth bared in final fear,
motionless on the concrete.

White cabbage moth,
wings flying flat and beautiful
on my windshield.

White and yellow cat,
fur catching afternoon sun,
I-70 past Columbia.

Something dark under vultures,
Blackwater, Missouri.
sparrows wheel away just in time.

Near Turner another stiff-legged dog,
a felled sparrow hawk,
wind lifting an empty wing.

Toward Lawrence
a dead coyote, yellow dog,
sun moving down flat and west.

Grackles lift off the road
rasping alarm,
dark shapes escaping into night sky.

Snakes

They fill the out-of-doors,
        their old cellophane skins
        left blowing in yellow grass,
        their holes unhidden beside creek beds.

We learn
        Beware of rocky outcrops.
        Don't flip flat stones.
        Stay away from old wells.

They pass busy nights—
        slipping wordless past sleeping dogs,
        stalking toads in the garden.
        Toward dawn
        they circle the back porch.

At the Natural History Museum
        we watch them eat mice
        one   slow   swallow
        and strike at glass.

We don't read Genesis
or Freud
or Aztec codices.

We watch where we step.

Gravity Follows Me from the Flint Hills

Flint layers flank this highway
broken only by erosion,
the Nemaha fault zone,
these asphalt roads.

Flint runs under
the El Dorado oil fields
and Bible belt fundamentalists
certain of Jesus
and Eternity.

Rinds of oceans and marshlands
settle under the prairies
tidy as piled rock fences.

Gravity, patient as the sun,
pulls at the next layer—
   Concrete, Asphalt, Lumber, Bricks.
   Concrete, Asphalt, Lumber, Bricks.

Stratification of Snow

*Not only is the universe inside our heads equal to the
physical universe in terms of the neurophysiological properties
involved—but the internal environment may be more real.*
Michael Talbot

Snow turns town into a gingerbread village
and my son Daniel says the snow
is crystals like quartz crystals.
I say yes and try to explain
how rocks and ice amount
to really the same thing.

G. calls and tap-dances stories
of shoveling five kinds of snow,
each layer an episode of cold or thaw,
and I say rocks and ice fall down the same—
I saw snow and limestone strata
on all the roads to Wichita last week,

and something else, too.
These words float around inside my head,
drift toward sentences

like those glass balls
full of water and miniature villages
you turn upside down and back
to make the snow fall
into carpets of white sparkles
so everything fits in your hands.

Spring Rain Runs

down the brick street
deeper in the middle,
an old creek bed,
and several blocks over
a gully meets the run-off
and carries the flood
past doghouses and clotheslines
behind frame houses,
rain sliding off
the roofs in sheets.
Shifts in the sidewalk
catch these cold drops
and behind the garage
a grassy puddle forms
under red tile eaves.

A few miles south
cattle drop calves—
one just born
lifted to its feet and fell,
unready for solid ground,
still floating in this rain.

Water collects in rounds,
reflects the shallow hip bones
and water in my flesh
hears, somehow hears,
and sees this chill, this rain.

Views of Kansas Highways

1. Mother's Day Drive

We head north, toward Lawrence,
into limestone country.
Highway slices stone,
exposing multitudes of skeletons,
hills filled with fossils—
crinoids, corals, clams.

Calcite
like these thick bones of mine
first formed grain by grain
from my mother's bloodstream.

Seedling cottonwoods
push up through rock cracks.
Layers of old ocean debris
hold up new spring grasses.

2. Toward Manhattan

Limestone blocks line the road
like walls of Assyrian fortresses.

We enter gates
to an old land
or hewn doors of hell—
the Great Desert.

Stacks of naked stones
mortared in place

follow us:
    black shale for old shallows, marshes,
    yellow limestone for sea bottoms.

Further below
peaks of the Nemaha Mountains
are buried in rain, wind, grit.
We pass carefully over the dead giant,
stepping on a grave.

At the center of the continent,
this New World,
lie frost-heaved rocks, sediment,
these ruins.

3. Matfield Green

The trees refuse to follow from Topeka.
The car radio loses contact
and mumbles fuzz to itself.

The highway bisects a moonscape
and you are completely alone.

If you see a diesel truck
it lumbers like a beast
lost from another age,
like you.

Two sounds rise from the gullies
and repetitious hills out there—
            in the summer
            wine and waves of cicada sounds.

            In the winter
            only yelps of wind.

4. West

Here the sky gives clarity to each tree—

a gray hand on the horizon,
perpendicular on horizontal.

The long slope of miles
approaching Colorado,
moving always into blue blue haze.

Each tree a slow traveler on this road.

Place

Is it the eagles returning to Lecompton, old Eagle Town,
that stretch of lookout cottonwoods on the Kaw River,

or is it those rivers we measure towns by,
where we wait for flood and drought tides?

Or finding my grandfather during a storm,
clouds and lightning and his face by the window?

Is it the house I grew up in,
the way the sun slanted through the front widow,
warm bars of winter dust and light?

Is it a locus inside a muddy muscle,
the heart squeezing rivulets of blood
again, again, again.

Gift of a Fossil Ammonite

for Eileen Williams

This sea creature,
Ram's Horn of Ammon,
still lugs its house,
the old empty rooms
turning around a center,
some chipped pearl still
cemented on the outside.

The stony shell held
a soft worm, attached
to its flat spire,
alone in an old Victorian home.

Crammed into the end
the soft body grew
squeezed out of the small center,
head end pushed forward
out of the shell casement.

Lost muscle is now fossil,
the casting coiled in its nest.
The echo body shows exactly
ridges and embroidered walls.

And no one knows, you say,
handing me this birthday gift,
why ammonites died out
leaving only one distant relation,
the nautilus.

We can choose whatever ending
to the story we want,
holding here, with wine and cake,

a frozen clock winding forward,
chamber by chamber,
a time line—its allotted seasons—
some 100 million years before ours.
Its dance we follow.

Small Town Landscapes
for Mary Swander

The county highway grids
and repeating stretches
of grass and cattle
hold people apart.
Gravel roads called "town"
branch off the black top.
The same gas station-beer hall-post office
appear every twenty miles,
their names gone as soon as spoken—
      Wilsey, Olpe, Allen.

Insurance calendars hung
in sheds mark a cycle
of high school football and harvest.
Each town of old families
immortalizes the few sires and dams:
swarthy German Catholics with green eyes
populate one quadrant,
round-faced blonds another.

In one place children have six toes
or half the town is twins,
matching potatoes in overalls.
Or a seed of Parkinson's disease
flourishes like wheat.
In this isolation
strains of genius are tolerated
equally with eccentrics.

People live in tumbling houses
surrounded by unmown weeds.

One of those barns contains antique violins,
another a tractor seat collection,
barbed wire displays, cattle skulls,
arrowheads arranged in sunflower patterns,
a vehicle pieced from a Harley and a Ford,
all secret in those wide open spaces.

The Oldest Continuous Civilization

We walk through the Shanghai Exhibit
with hushed grandmothers and scholars.
Potted bamboos mark dim pathways
and lights burnish the specimens.
Chinese flute music fades and resumes
like moments of imagination.

Leisurely, we pace the map of time,
ten minutes for the Chou Dynasty,
half a room for the T'ang.
Illumined charts of the dynasties
appear and recede.
Charts trace generations of cities,
shifts of races and trade routes.

Bronze vessels, paintings,
jade, ivory, and porcelain
fit silhouettes traced on timelines,
cloak of text around each object.

We pause at the largest display:
Funerary figurines march five meters
under glass—giant chess pieces
of slave women, guards, and horsemen—
and death is as ordered
as our stroll through galleries.

A fluorescent-bright sales room comes last
like a burst of organ music after church
Among ceramic horses, paper cutouts,
our museum procession disperses,
the oldest continuous civilization behind us.

Sycamore: A Removal

It dropped huge-handed leaves
over the garden
and long peelings of tan bark.
White tree skin underneath
matched the snow.

After the tree cutters leave,
a new silence.
The sky presses into the fence
and unfamiliar houses
appear in the distance.
The sun practices new angles.

Dragon Kite, 1981

The series of poems that came to be published as the chapbook *Dragon Kite* began in poetry workshops with Victor Contoski at the University of Kansas. I took three or four classes with him during the late 1970's.

Contoski nurtured his students with practical advice about the publishing world. One evening he showed us his book *Broken Treaties*, and he said each poem in the book had been rejected at least ten times. This heartened every student. His highest praise for a poem was that it was "publishable," and he would direct students to submit to particular editors. He made it clear that writing was a public act—and also a political act. I do not think that I would have continued writing without his kindness and practical direction.

Contoski stressed that a book of poems should have overall coherence. I had begun a series of poems about my children and their grandparents, Kim Quong Low and Thuey Kin (Mary) Low. I interviewed my in-laws, who lived in Salina, Kansas, and some of these conversations were in the original chapbook. I have omitted them here because they are more prose than poetry.

Dan Jaffe of BookMark Press (UMKC) saw the original manuscript of forty pages and cut it to twenty. I remember sitting with him in a Westport restaurant where he announced this editing with a flourish. Now I am grateful for his wisdom. He published *Dragon Kite* in *Mid-America Trio,* along with chapbooks by Stan Banks and Greg Field, who have continued as friends in the Kansas City writing community.

from Dragon Kite

Looking for Your Blue Spot
for David

We always heard
Asian babies have blue spots,
blue splotches of pigment
on their bottoms,
so at your first bath
we turned you over.

There glowed a blue quarter
at the base of your spine
like a scar
where someone snipped off your tail
and higher up your back
        indigo Madagascar
                floated alone.

These blue markings grew,
stretched out
bath by bath
until invisible
except for a certain sheen.

Now we play the game
        Where is your blue spot?

You grab your pants
and run giggling through the hall.
        Has it moved to your elbow?
        Has it moved to your neck?
You shout back
        It's looking for someone else!

Jade

The stone nearest heaven
takes many forms:

pebbles in Burmese streams,
mottled or solid,
dark nephrite and lavender jadeite
and rust, yellow, white,
sea green, apple green,
the rarest translucent.

Pierced and set in gold
it is heaven
next to the skin:
a bracelet of seven stones
reaching like a rainbow
around the wrist
or pendants shaped
into peaches or the Buddha
to endure each color of day.

In a lifetime
skin polishes the stone.
Body heat continues the work
of heaven and sky.

Sleeping Eurasian
  for Daniel

Your father's big ears remain hidden
behind freckles and sun burn.
Only in a swimming dunking or this daylight nap
do those ears stick out,
long and deep-lobed as the Buddha's ears.

You listen in your sleep
for toads out the back door,
Kansas crickets, and
airplane drone beyond the trees.

Will you hear your ear-secret,
memories your grandparents left across the ocean?

Ming Bowl

Flowers:

fine blue lines
circling together
never touching

tracing
the simple
rice bowl

two hundred years old

rim open
to catch clouds.

Quilting, 1984

The *Quilting* poems developed from a time when my mother began handing down family quilts—one from her maternal grandmother Charlotte Root Bruner, and two from my father's paternal grandmother, Mary Scott Dotson. Both had lived in central Kansas. Charlotte and her husband Frank grew up in the Burns area; Mary Dotson grew up in a sod house near Newton.

I met my great-grandmother Dotson once, when I was about two, and I remember the respect my parents had for her. Even as a small child, I felt awed by her kind demeanor. My mother gave me her fan quilt when I set up housekeeping in Lawrence. It had never been used. I felt great conflict about whether I should save it for my own children, or use it. I finally did use it for awhile, and I resolved the conflict by learning to quilt myself. I also hoped to honor the quilts—and the lives of my grandmothers—with these poems.

When Linda Samson Talleur approached me in 1983 for some poems she could use for a fine press edition, I gave her the *Quilting* poems, and she commissioned hand-made paper for the project. The paper had a high rag content, and pieces of cotton fabric were added to the mixture. Samson Talleur designed six vivid broadsides, which fit within a cloth-covered box. This amazing, handmade artwork is in the Spencer Museum at the University of Kansas and many private collections. An edition of about a hundred were made, and a few are still available in 1999.

from **Quilting**

Quiltmaker

Great-grandmother Dotson,
the sodhouse settler I met once
and never forgot—
"A daughter of Isaiah and Harriet Sinks Scott
        Born January 17, 1869 at Dayton, Ohio."

This rainy afternoon
I open her quilts on my bed—
    Flower Garden, rosettes of white and green;
    Wedding Ring, locking circles of pink;
    Grandma's Fan, plumes of blue and red.

"Stricken dead after visiting all evening with friends,
        Newton, Kansas, 1954."

I remember the taste of cream pie.

I remember her diary:
        "I suffer today from rose fever."
        "Today we have a healthy girl baby."

I look in the dresser mirror and see:
        her quilts spread behind me
        her brown eyes looking back.

Wedding Ring Quilt
after a quilt by Charlotte Root Bruner

The tiniest rectangles arch
into overlapping circles—

      pink-and-white
      ruby-and-white

unbroken rounds
like wedding bands.

Husband
we awaken within circles of sunlight.

Every morning
I come back to you

walk out of dreams
into soft sheets and your soft skin.

I return to steady breathing
our steady daily hunger.

Blue-and-White Quilt

1.
The quilt airs on the line
its colors fresh as Ming chinaware:
      blue triangles
      white squares blowing
      together a pattern
      called Bear Claw.

The banner rolls in wind.
Diamonds shift into paws.

Blue sky and blue cotton:
panes bordered by white sills:

      Look into.

2.
      Tonight
      we piece together birdsong
      and damp evening air
      like memory.

Talking together like this
cheese and strawberries
on the table
a new pattern
pulls together.

      Blue-and-white quilt
      still skims sky.

The Quilt, Again

Mend the frayed edges.
Cover up loose stuffing.

Bring back the day I unfolded it—

    crisp white cotton
    bright flower-dress colors

    handed down by gentle ghosts
    women finishing their lives
    still doing for others

    still stitching around, around
    until time comes to put down
    white thread and retire.

I want this warmth
spread over me each night.

DENISE LOW is the 2007–2009 Kansas poet laureate. She has been a professor and administrator at Haskell Indian Nations University since 1984 and a visiting professor at the University of Richmond. She received a PhD from the University of Kansas and an MFA in Creative Writing from Wichita State University. She has won awards from the National Endowment for the Humanities, The Newberry Library, The Lannan Foundation, Academy of American Poets-Pami Jurassi Bush, Roberts Foundation. She has published books, articles, and reviews about poetry, Indigenous American literature, Langston Hughes, Cheyenne pictographic ledger art, and interstices between culture and the natural world.

She and Thomas Pecore Weso publish and distribute books through Mammoth Publications. Her blog is deniselow.blogspot.com.

.